W9-DEH-164

GREAT AFRICAN-AMERICAN WOMEN

Oprah Winfrey

Heather C. Hudak

WEIGL PUBLISHERS INC.

Published by Weigl Publishers Inc.
350 5th Avenue, Suite 3304, PMB 6G
New York, NY USA 10118-0069
Web site: www.weigl.com

B
WIN

Library of Congress Cataloging-in-Publication Data

Hudak, Heather C., 1975-
  Oprah Winfrey / Heather C. Hudak.
    p. cm. -- (Great African American women)
  Includes index.
  ISBN 1-59036-335-3 (hard cover : alk. paper) -- ISBN 1-59036-341-8 (soft cover : alk. paper)
  1. Winfrey, Oprah--Juvenile literature. 2. Television personalities--United States--Juvenile literature. 3. Actors--United States--Juvenile literature. 4. African American television personalities--Juvenile literature. 5. African American actors--Juvenile literature. I. Title. II. Series.
  PN1992.4.W56H84 2005
  791.4502'8'092--dc22

                           2004029959

Printed and bound in the United States of America
1 2 3 4 5 6 7 8 9 0   09 08 07 06 05

Project Coordinator Janice L. Redlin
Copy Editor Heather Kissock
Photo Research Kim Winiski and Annalise Bekkering
Design Terry Paulhus **Layout** Kathryn Livingstone

Photograph Credits
Every reasonable effort has been made to trace ownership and to obtain permission to reprint copyright material. The publishers would be pleased to have any errors or omissions brought to their attention so that they may be corrected in subsequent printings.

Cover: Oprah Winfrey is known for her acting roles, her skills as a businessperson, and hosting her own talk show.

Cover: Getty Images/Vince Bucci (front); Getty Images/Spencer Platt (back); **Getty Images:** pages 1 (Frank Micelotta), 3 (Vince Bucci), 4 (Peter Kramer), 5 (Getty Images), 6T (Kevin Winter), 6B (Ira Block/National Geographic), 7TL (Comstock Images), 7R (Raymond Gehman/National Geographic), 7BL (Bill Colgin), 9 (Harpo Productions), 10 (Comstock Images/Getty Images), 11 (William Thomas Cain), 12 (George Burns/Harpo Productions), 13TL (Tannen Maury/AFP), 13TR (Kevin Winter), 13B (Michael Tullberg), 14 (John Livzey), 15L (Scott Olson/AFP), 15R (Scott Olson), 16L (Steve Kagan/Time Life Pictures), 16R (Kevin Horan/Time Life Pictures), 17 (Tammie Arroyo), 18 (Kevin Winter), 19T (STR/AFP), 19B (Carlo Allegri), 20 (Touchstone Pictures), 21L (Spencer Platt), 21R (Tim Graham), 22T (Siede Preis), 22TM (C Squared Studios), 22M (Ryan McVay), 22BM (Siede Preis), 22B (Digital Vision); **Photos.com:** page 8.

Oprah Winfrey

CONTENTS

Who is Oprah Winfrey?

O prah Winfrey is one of the world's most **successful businesswomen**. She leads a company called Harpo Productions. The company was created in 1988. It promotes Oprah's image as a well-known talk-show host, actress, and spokesperson. She owns *O, The Oprah Magazine*. Oprah also owns a television and Internet network called Oxygen Media. She uses her fame to help charities and people around the world. In 1997, Oprah started Oprah's Angel Network. This company helps others in need. Oprah has won many awards for her work on and off screen. She has become an **inspiration** to people all over the world.

You only have to believe that you can succeed, that you can be whatever your heart desires, be willing to work for it, and you can have it.

Growing Up in Kosciusko

Oprah was born on January 29, 1954, in Kosciusko, Mississippi. Her parents, Vernita Lee and Vernon Winfrey, were not married. They were not ready to raise a child, so Oprah lived on a farm with her grandmother. Oprah and her grandmother had very little money. Oprah did not have toys or friends to play with. She enjoyed reading and writing stories. Oprah gave speeches at church. She was very smart and skipped grades one and two. Oprah moved to Milwaukee, Wisconsin, when she was 6 years old. Here, Oprah lived with her mother, who worked as a housecleaner. Oprah and her mother lived in a run-down apartment.

The Mississippi River is an important body of water in Oprah's home state. The United States ships 60 percent of its exported grain via the Mississippi River.

MISSISSIPPI Tidbits

 FLAG

 SEAL

 **BIRD** Mockingbird

  TREE Magnolia

 FLOWER Magnolia

MISSISSIPPI

★ Kosciusko
★ **Jackson**

In 1914, the first female rural mail carrier in the United States delivered mail by buggy in Mississippi.

The Mississippi River is the largest river in the United States. It is the nation's main waterway and is nicknamed Old Man River.

In 1963, the medical center at the University of Mississippi completed the world's first human lung **transplant**. In 1964, it performed the world's first heart transplant.

Mississippi is the home of North America's rarest cranes. Sandhill cranes live in Mississippi's grassy savannas.

The world's largest cottonwood tree plantation is located in Mississippi.

Think about it!

How might living in the state of Mississippi have influenced Oprah? Research your state's sites and symbols, and write about how they might have influenced you and your family.

Mississippi became the twentieth state of the United States on December 10, 1817.

Studying Speech and Acting

When Oprah was 14 years old, her mother sent her to live with her father in Nashville, Tennessee. Vernon helped Oprah earn good grades at school. Oprah's grades won her a school trip to the White House. A local radio station talked to her about the trip. They liked Oprah's voice and hired her to host a radio show. Oprah began her radio career at 16 years of age.

Radio hosts must speak well and be organized. They also must know how to operate studio equipment.

Later, Oprah studied speech and acting at Tennessee State University. She also won two beauty contests. These successes helped Oprah earn a job as a television news reporter. She was the first African-American woman to work as a news reporter in Nashville. Soon, Oprah moved to Baltimore, Maryland. She became co-host of the morning talk show *People Are Talking*. Oprah worked on the show for 8 years.

Many well-known people, including First Lady Laura Bush, have appeared with Oprah on *The Oprah Winfrey Show*.

oprah winfrey QUICK Facts

A spelling mistake on Oprah's birth certificate changed her name from Orpah to Oprah. Orpah comes from the Book of Ruth in the Bible.

The only women who owned production studios before Oprah were actresses Mary Pickford and Lucille Ball.

The Harpo Productions company name is Oprah's name spelled backward.

Oprah's speaking abilities won her a 4-year scholarship to Tennessee State University.

Oprah moved to Chicago in 1984. There, she hosted a talk show called *A.M. Chicago*. Soon after, Oprah played the role of Sofia in the movie *The Color Purple*. She earned an **Academy Award nomination** for her acting. In 1986, Oprah began working on her own talk show. On *The Oprah Winfrey Show*, Oprah talked about her life. The show was a success and earned Oprah respect and wealth. With her money, she bought the show from the American Broadcasting Company (ABC) and started Harpo Productions. Oprah became the third woman in history to own a major production studio. *The Oprah Winfrey Show* earns millions of dollars each year. Oprah has become the richest African-American woman in the United States.

Public Speaking

Reading, writing, public speaking, and business sense were important to Oprah's success. She was a talented speaker at a very young age. By age 3, Oprah was reciting Bible verses at her grandmother's church. Oprah also enjoyed reading. It allowed her to use her imagination to escape her poor living conditions. Later, Oprah used stories from her troubled life to relate to her viewers. She talked about her problems, failures, and fears on television.

Oprah took her studies seriously. She earned good grades in school. Oprah won a public-speaking contest in her teens. This success earned her money for a **college** education. Oprah practiced public speaking, worked hard, and **invested** her money wisely.

By 1999, Oprah was teaching university courses. She and her partner, Stedman Graham, taught business courses at Northwestern University.

Public Speaking Rules

Public speakers must:

- ☑ prepare and practice the material
- ☑ speak loudly, clearly, and confidently
- ☑ make eye contact with the audience
- ☑ communicate their interest for the subject to the audience
- ☑ not read to the audience; refer to the material occasionally, but try to be **spontaneous**
- ☑ not share everything they know about the subject; too much material could bore the audience
- ☑ make sure there is time for questions from the audience

Many of Oprah's awards, including the Marian Anderson Award, are for the work she does helping people.

What is a Talk Show?

On a talk show, hosts ask well-known or interesting people to answer questions. There is no **script** for the show. Guests talk about their lives.

Producing a talk show is not easy. Many people work together to create each show. First, there must be an idea for the show. Next, someone must contact guests to appear on the show.

The lighting crew aims bright lights at the host and guests. A sound crew makes sure the host and guests have microphones. The camera crew films the show. These are just a few of the people who help produce each show.

Many people work behind the scenes to book guests, such as Arnold Schwarzenegger and Maria Shriver, for Oprah's television show.

Talk shows present many different topics to viewers. They often explore issues and values that society is questioning at the time. Oprah has discussed a range of subjects in her role as a talk-show host.

News

On news talk shows, reporters or **anchors** talk to people about current issues and events. One example of a news talk-show host is **LARRY KING**.

ELLEN DEGENERES hosts an entertainment talk show. Guests are most often actors or musicians. These shows sometimes have silly **skits** and funny speeches.

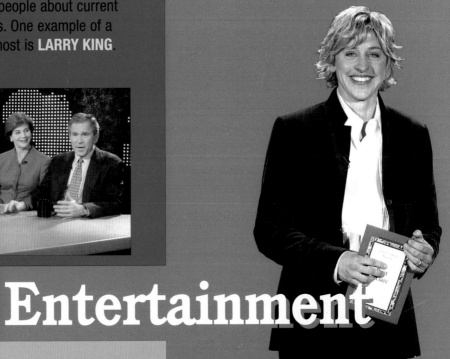

Entertainment

News and Entertainment

News and entertainment talk shows have guests who are either in the news or are entertainers. Often, the hosts of these shows have worked as news reporters. Oprah hosts a news and entertainment talk show. Her guests include actors and war victims. BARBARA WALTERS is a news and entertainment talk-show host.

Chicago, Illinois, Highlights

Chicago has been called "the pulse of America." It has tall buildings, big businesses, and millions of people. Chicago has many **museums**, restaurants, and sporting events. It is also known for its live music clubs. Wrigley Field is home to the Cubs, Chicago's major league baseball team. People travel from all over the world to see *The Oprah Winfrey Show*, too.

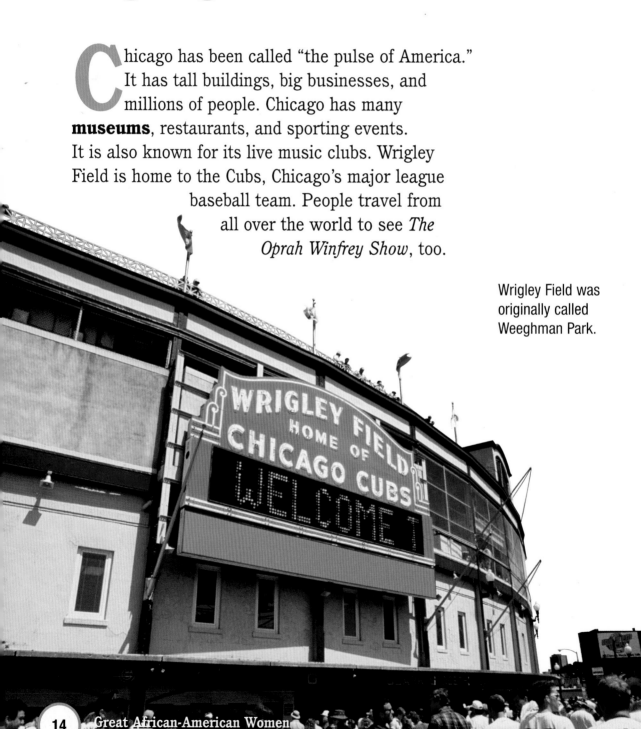

Wrigley Field was originally called Weeghman Park.

Chicago
Quick Facts

Nicknames: Windy City, Second City, Garden City

Claim to Fame: Sears Tower
The Sears Tower is the tallest building in North America. It stands at 1,450 feet (440 meters) and is 110 stories high. From the Skydeck, tourists can see 40 to 50 miles (64 to 80 kilometers) on a clear day.

Baseball: Wrigley Field
Wrigley Field was built in 1914. It was built on the grounds of a **seminary**. The stadium can seat almost 40,000 people. Well-known baseball players, such as Babe Ruth, Pete Rose, and Sammy Sosa, have hit many home runs at Wrigley Field.

The Sears Tower has two antennas on the top of the building. The antennas increase the height of the Sears Tower to 1,725 feet (525 m).

Chicago was built in the early 1800s. In 1871, the city burned down, but it was quickly rebuilt. By 1900, nearly 2 million people lived in Chicago. Today, Chicago has a population of almost 3 million people. Chicago is home to some of the world's best-known buildings, such as the Chicago Water Tower, the John Hancock Center, and the Sears Tower.

Overcoming Obstacles

As a child, Oprah was **abused**. Reading books made Oprah feel better. She put her troubles aside and focused on school. Oprah believed she could become a successful person.

Oprah attended college in the 1970s. At this time, few African Americans went to college. African Americans were not always given the opportunities that other people had.

Television stations worried people would not watch an African-American anchor. Viewers enjoyed watching Oprah. She was honest and open about her feelings. This helped Oprah become a successful talk-show host.

Oprah has been very open about her weight problems. She connects with many people because of her openness.

Oprah has struggled to lose weight. **Nutritionists**, diet experts, and gym trainers have helped Oprah learn to control her weight. She has learned to be happy with her size, as long as she is healthy. Viewers appreciate that Oprah shares their problems with weight loss and gain.

In the 1990s, many talk shows featured topics that shocked audiences and created conflict. These shows were very popular. Oprah did not want to change her show. The ratings for *The Oprah Winfrey Show* dropped. Over time, people began to appreciate Oprah's approach.

Oprah follows a diet and exercise program to help her control her weight and to stay healthy.

Special Achievements

In kindergarten, Oprah wrote a letter to her teacher asking to skip a grade. The next day, Oprah began grade one. Later, she skipped grade two. At 19, Oprah became the youngest television news anchor and the first female African-American anchor at a television station in Nashville.

Oprah won the Bob Hope Humanitarian Award in 2002 for her contributions to broadcasting.

Oprah has won many important awards, including The George Foster Peabody Individual Achievement Award. This is an important broadcasting award. She received the IRTS Gold Medal Award from the International Radio & Television Society in 1996. This award is presented for success in the electronic-media industry. Oprah received the National Academy of Television Arts & Sciences' Lifetime Achievement Award. In 2001, *Newsweek* magazine named Oprah "Woman of the Century." *TIME* magazine has called Oprah one of the 100 most **influential** people of the twentieth century.

Oprah's Angel Network helps many people in Africa.

More than 25 million American viewers watch *The Oprah Winfrey Show* each day. It is the top-rated talk show in television history. Oprah and the show have won dozens of **Emmy Awards**. The show is seen in 112 countries. In 1996, Oprah began Oprah's Book Club to encourage people to read more often. Each book featured by the club has become a bestseller. Oprah's Angel Network urges people to **donate** to those in need. The network has received many donations. The money is used to help people pay for college and to build homes and schools.

Oprah pays for the care of five South-African children. She also plans to build twelve schools in Africa. The first school was built near Johannesburg, South Africa. It is a school for girls.

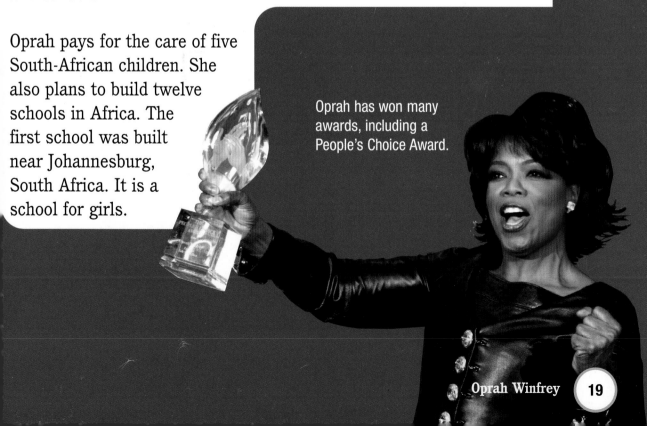

Oprah has won many awards, including a People's Choice Award.

Oprah in the Media

Oprah is on television every weekday. She makes many other public appearances, too. In 1986, Oprah acted in the movie *Native Son*. She played herself in the 1987 film *Throw Momma from the Train*. Oprah acted in the 1998 movie *Beloved*. She has also appeared on television shows and movies, such as *The Women of Brewster Place*.

Oprah played the role of Sethe in *Beloved*, alongside Danny Glover.

Many magazines print stories about Oprah. She has been featured in *Essence, Vogue, Newsweek, People,* and *InStyle*. Oprah is often written about in tabloid magazines, too.

In 2001, Oprah took her show on the road. The Live Your Best Life Tour brought Oprah to many cities. She held workshops to help women take control of their lives. Oprah also appears at other events. Some are charity events. Others are award shows.

Time Line

DECADE	OPRAH WINFREY	WORLD EVENTS
1950s	Oprah is born on January 29, 1954, in Kosciusko, Mississippi.	In 1954, the United States Supreme Court bans **racial segregation** in public schools.
1960s	In 1968, Oprah's mother sends her to live with her father in Nashville, Tennessee.	In 1968, civil rights leader Martin Luther King, Jr., is killed in Memphis, Tennessee.
1970s	Oprah becomes a morning talk-show host in Baltimore, Maryland, in 1977.	In 1977, fifteen countries, including the United States, sign a pact to stop producing nuclear weapons.
1980s	In 1986, Oprah starts hosting a talk show called *The Oprah Winfrey Show*.	The spacecraft, *Voyager 2*, discovers new information about the planet Uranus in 1986.
1990s	In 1996, Oprah begins Oprah's Book Club.	In 1996, Prince Charles and Princess Diana of Great Britain divorce after 15 years of marriage.
2000s	Oprah creates *O, The Oprah Magazine* in 2000. In 2001, *Newsweek* magazine names Oprah "Woman of the Century."	The presidents of North and South Korea sign a peace agreement in 2000 that ends 50 years of poor relations. The World Trade Center is destroyed in New York City on September 11, 2001.

Start a Book Club

Oprah's Book Club has thousands of members worldwide. Oprah selects a book she would like others to read. Then, she sets a date to talk about the book on television. Some people have book clubs in their neighborhood. You can start your own book club.

1. Get together with your friends, and select a book you would like to read.

2. Talk to your friends about the book. Then, make a sign telling people when you will meet. Use paper and crayons to make the sign. Make sure you include the time, date, place, and book name. Tape the sign on a wall where people will see it.

3. Read the book. Write notes as you read. This will help you remember what you read.

4. Meet with the group. Talk about what you learned from the book.

Materials

your favorite book
paper
crayons
tape

Now you have found a fun way to share your interest in reading with your friends.

Further Research

Further Reading

Blashfield, Jean F. *Oprah Winfrey*. Milwaukee, WI: World Almanac Library, 2002.

Raatma, Lucia. *Oprah Winfrey: Entertainer, Producer, and Businesswoman*. New York, NY: Ferguson Publishing Company, 2001.

Stone, Tanya Lee. *Oprah Winfrey: Success with an Open Heart*. Minneapolis, MN: Millbrook Press, 2001.

Web Sites

To learn more about Oprah's life and career, log on to these sites.

Academy of Achievement
www.achievement.org/autodoc/
page/win0bio-1

A Fan's Web Site on Oprah
www.oprahwinfrey.de

Harpo Productions, Inc.
www.oprah.com

Words to Know

abused: to be hurt or injured

Academy Award nomination: being chosen to run for an acting award for movie performers and producers

anchors: people that host programs

businesswomen: women who do business or work for a company

college: a school of higher learning that people attend after high school

donate: to give to a good cause

Emmy Awards: awards for television performers

influential: having or exercising power

inspiration: something that moves a person to create

invested: spent money on something in the hope of making more money

museums: buildings where collections that are important to art, history, or science are kept and shown to people

nutritionists: people who help others learn to eat healthy

racial segregation: separation by race

script: the written version of a play or a movie intended for an audience

seminary: a school for students studying to be priests or ministers

skits: short, funny plays

spontaneous: to do something without planning

successful: having reached a wanted goal

transplant: medically move an organ from one person to another person

Index

DATE DUE

MAY 0 3 2007			
NOV 2 1			
FEB 1 9 2008			
NOV 0 2 2010			
MAR 0 4 2011			

B
WIN

Hudak, Heather
Oprah Winfrey

DEMCO